AMAZING ME

FOREWARD

In a world where representation matters more than ever, this affirmation coloring and tracing journal serves as a vibrant celebration of the strength, beauty, and resilience of minority girls. Each page is designed not just to inspire creativity, but also to empower
young minds with bible verses and positive affirmations that resonate deeply with their unique experiences.
As you color, remember that each stroke represents not only your creativity but also your identity. This book is a space where you can express yourself freely, explore your thoughts, and embrace the incredible power within you. The affirmations chosen reflect the rich tapestry of cultures, experiences, and dreams that shape who you are.
May this journal be a source of joy, reflection, and empowerment. Let it remind you that you are worthy, capable, and deserving of all the beautiful things life has to offer.
Happy coloring!

I am strong,
courageous,
and not afraid,
for the Lord
my God is with me.
(Deuteronomy 31:6)

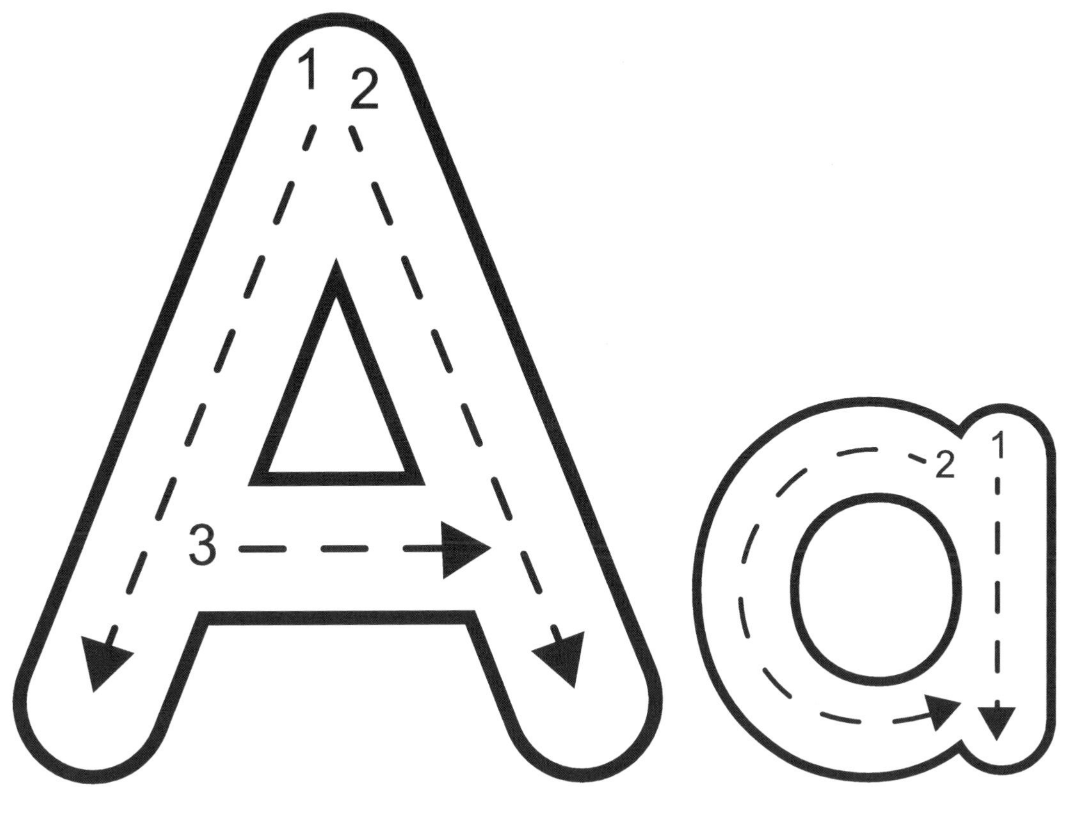

Aa

I am amazing!

I am amazing!

I am amazing!

I am active!

I am active!

I am active!

I AM BLESSED
TO BE A BLESSING
TO OTHERS.
(GENESIS 12:2)

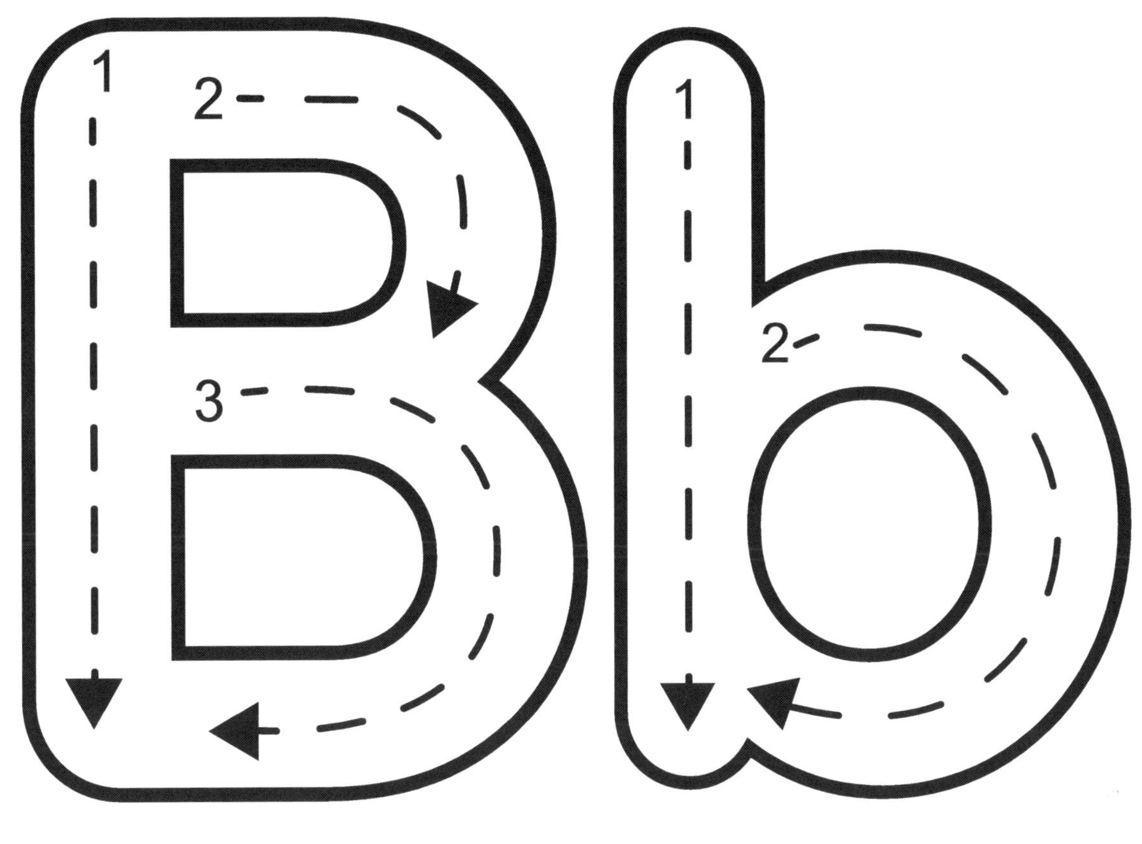

B b B b B b B b

B b B b B b B b

B b B b B b B b

I am brave!

I am brave!

I am brave!

I am bold!
I am bold!
I am bold!

I am more
than a conqueror
Through Him who
loves me.
(Romans 8:37)

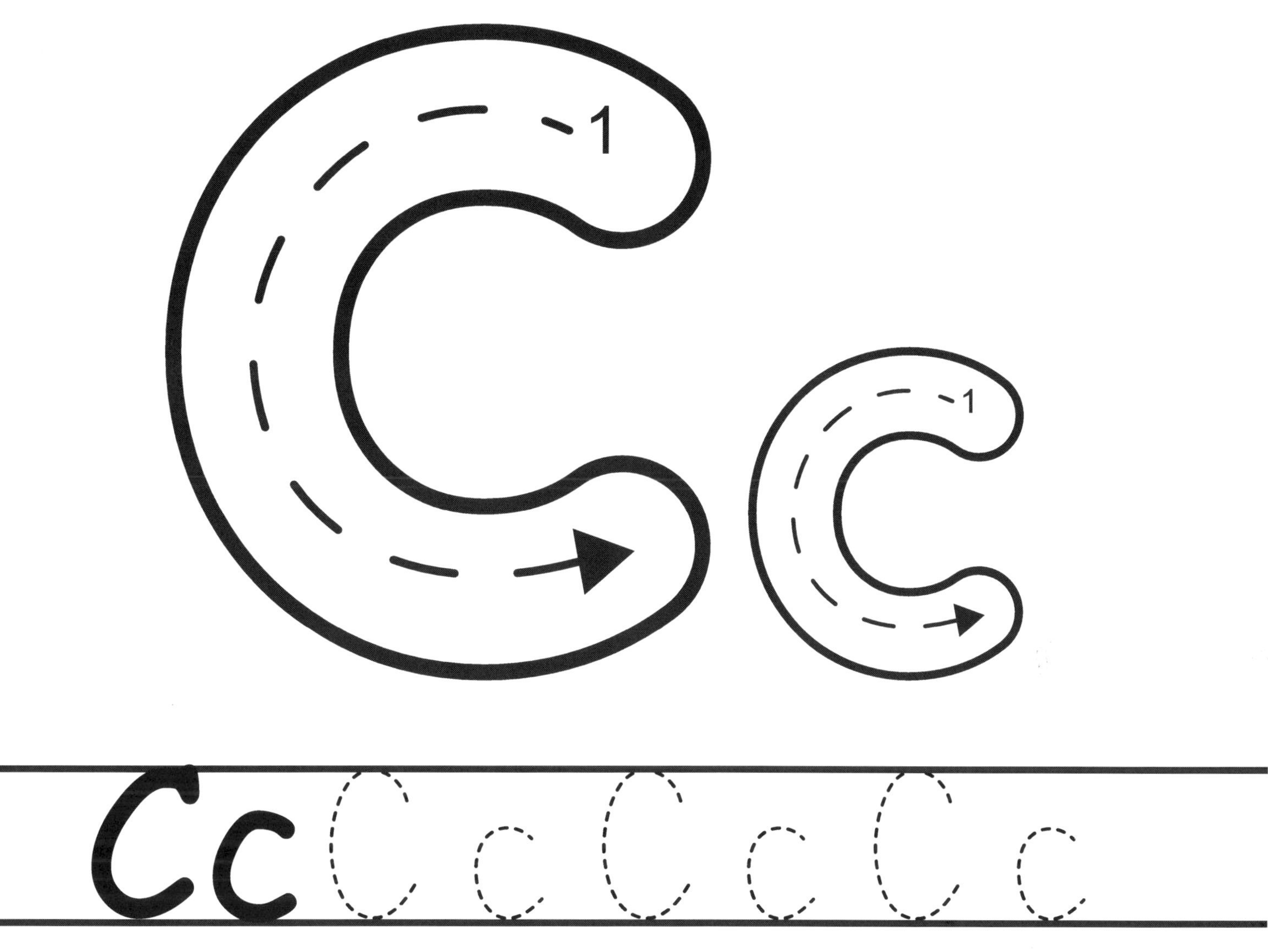

Cc

I am creative!

I am creative!

I am creative!

I am caring!

I am caring!

I am caring!

I am blessed when
I trust in the Lord
and make Him
my hope.
(Jeremiah 17:7)

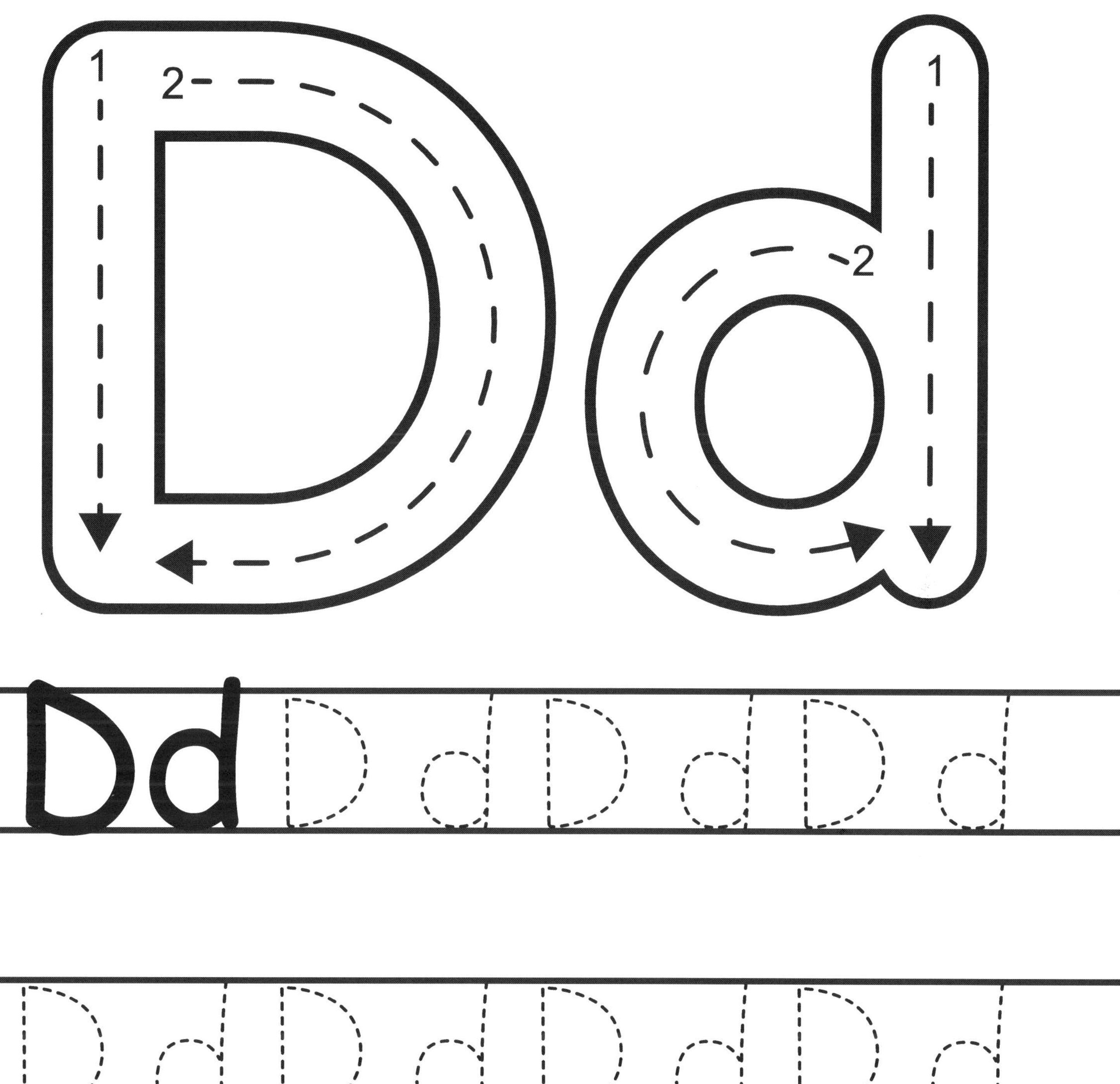
1
2
2
1
Dd

I am dynamic!

I am dynamic!

I am dynamic!

I am dependable!

I am dependable!

I am dependable!

I AM LOVED
WITH AN
EVERLASTING LOVE.
(JEREMIAH 31:3)

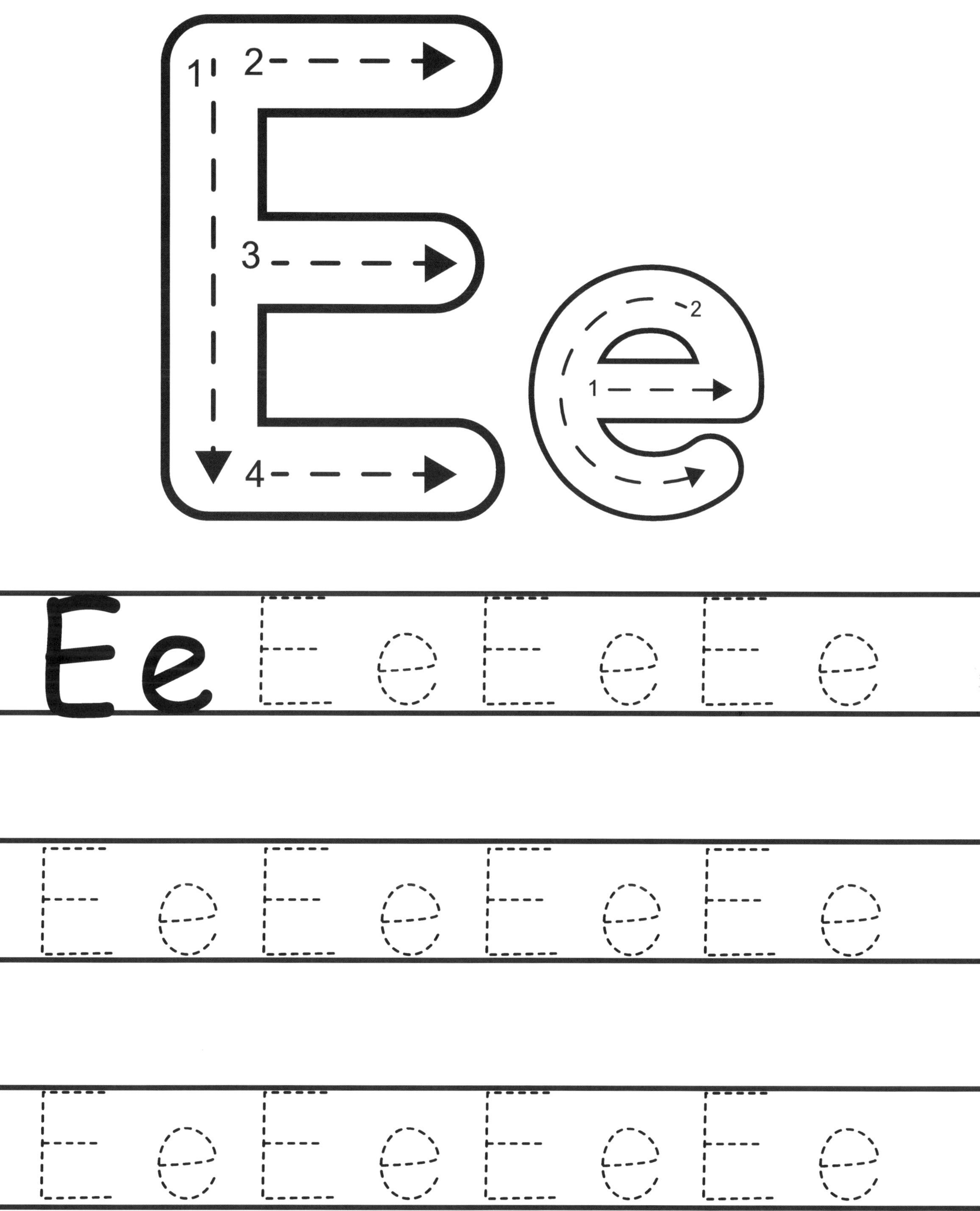

1
2
3
4
1
2
Ee

I am energetic!

I am energetic!

I am energetic!

I am excellent!

I am excellent!

I am excellent!

I am redeemed and forgiven through the blood of Jesus. (Ephesians 1:7)

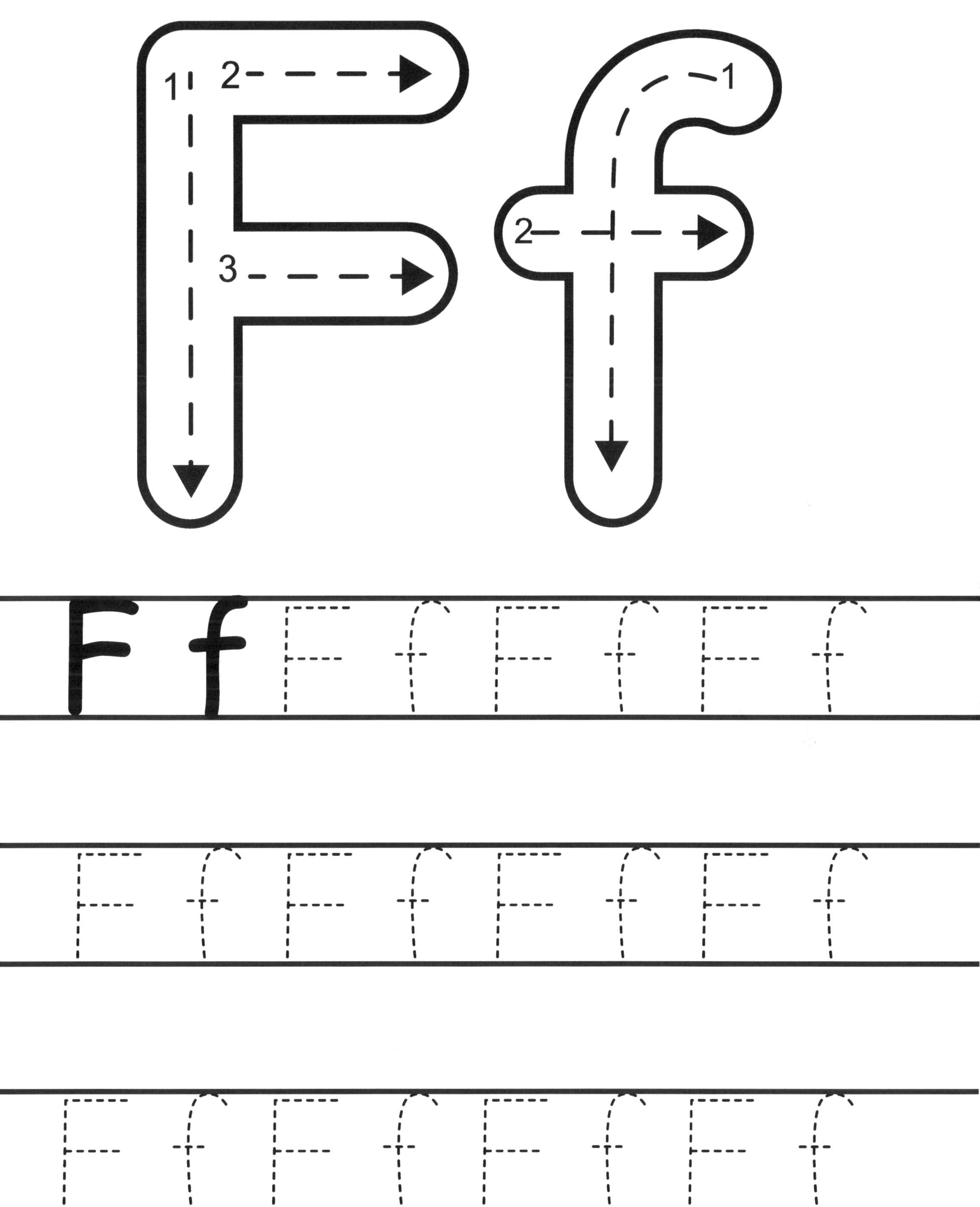

1
2
3
1
2
F f

I am fabulous!

I am fabulous!

I am fabulous!

I am friendly!
I am friendly!
I am friendly!

I AM FILLED WITH
HOPE AND EXPECTATION
IN THE LORD.
(PSALM 62:5)

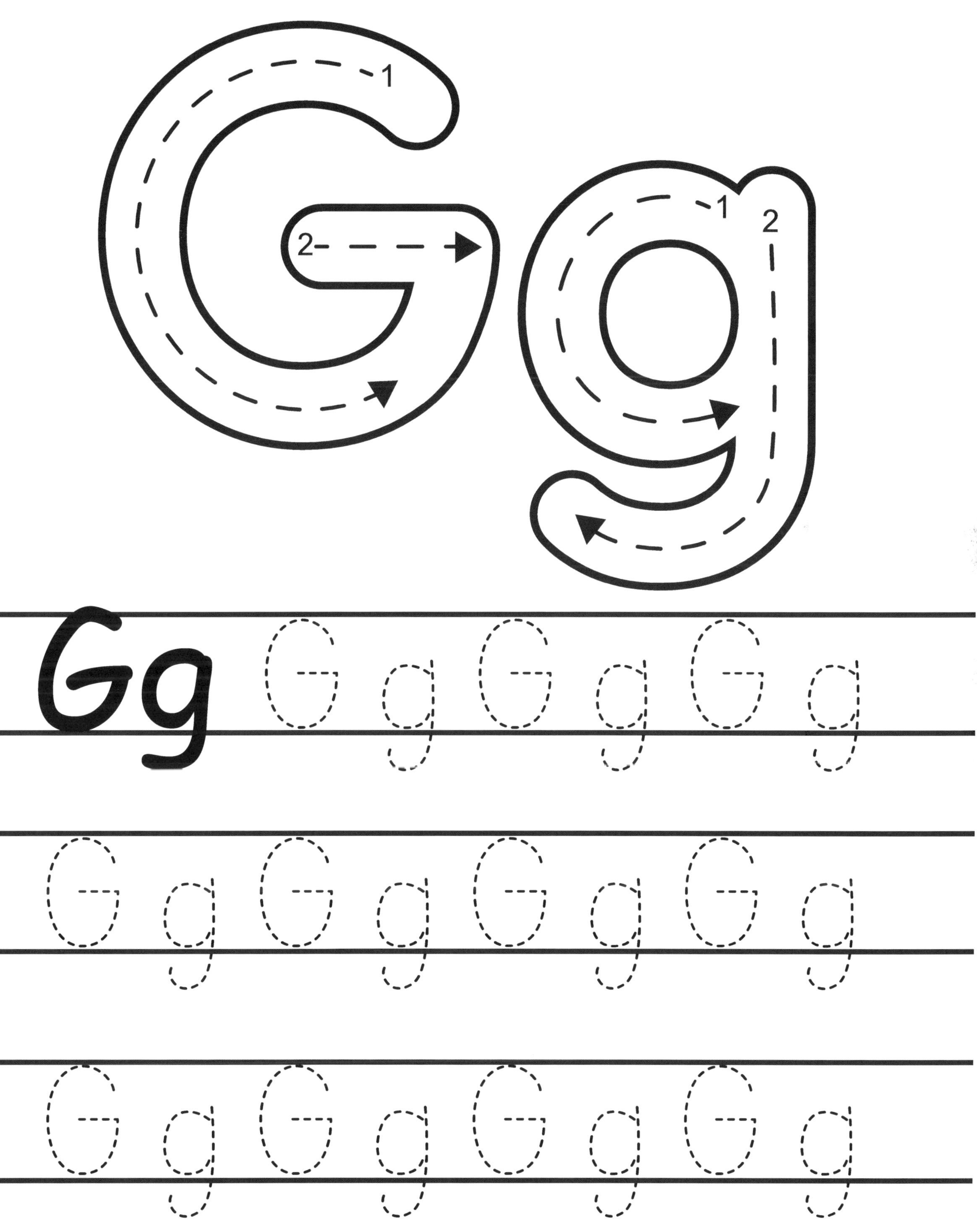
1
2
1
2
Gg

I am a gift!
I am a gift!
I am a gift!

I am genuine!

I am genuine!

I am genuine!

I AM THE HEAD
AND NOT THE TAIL,
ABOVE AND
NOT BENEATH.
(DEUTERONOMY 28:13)

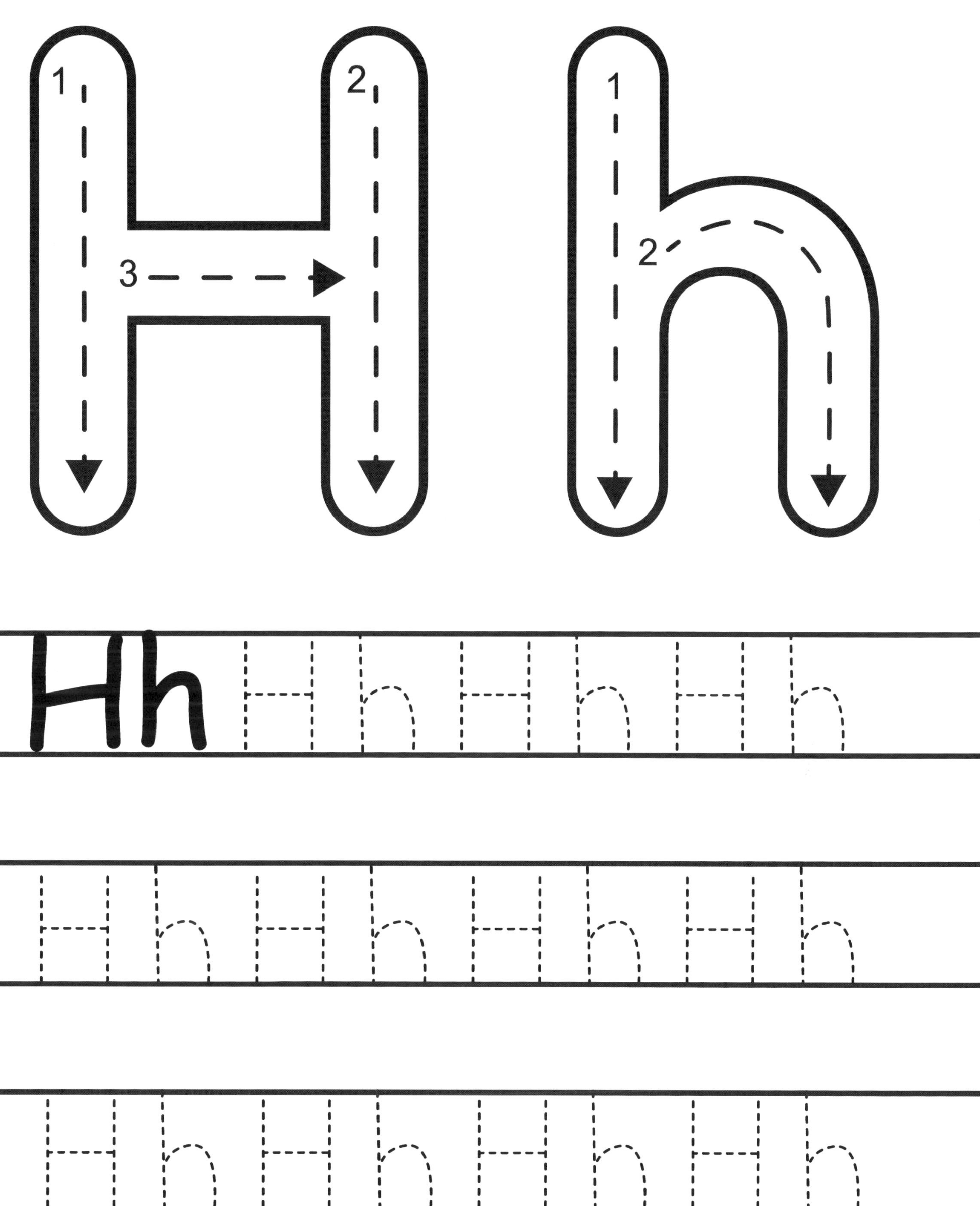
1
2
3
1
2
Hh

I am helpful!

I am helpful!

I am helpful!

I am humble!

I am humble!

I am humble!

I AM PATIENT
AND HAVE PEACE,
KNOWING THAT GOD'S
TIMING IS PERFECT.
(ECCLESIASTES 3:11)

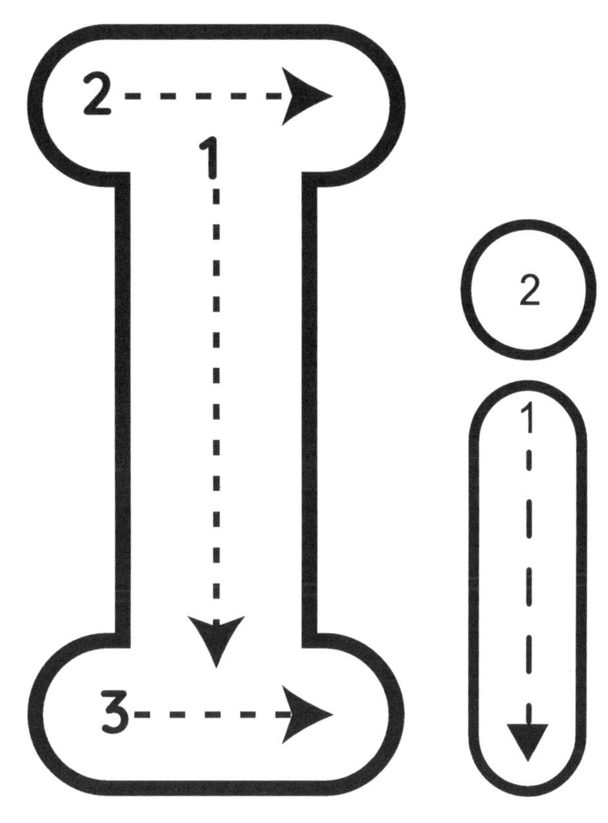
2
1
3
2
1

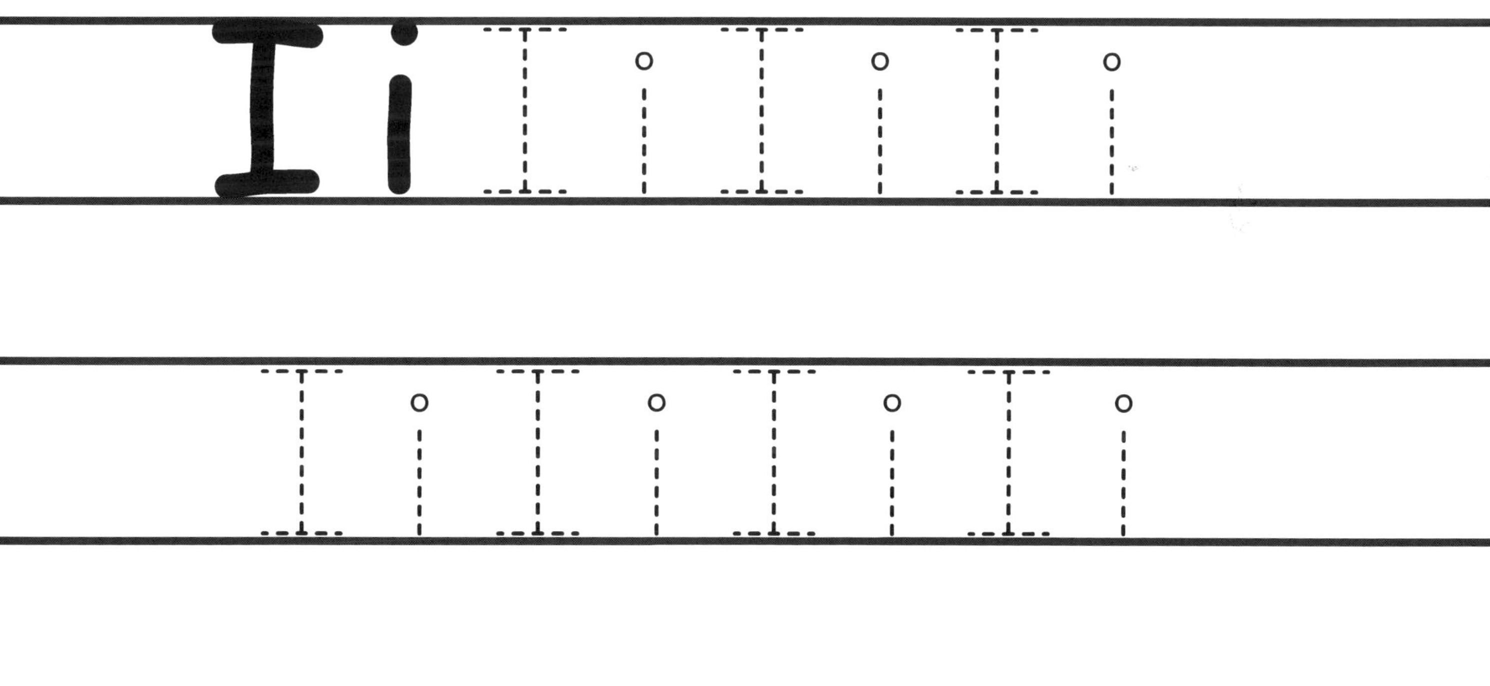
I i

I am intelligent!

I am intelligent!

I am intelligent!

I am important!

I am important!

I am important!

I am a friend
of Jesus, and He
laid down His
life for me.
(John 15:13)

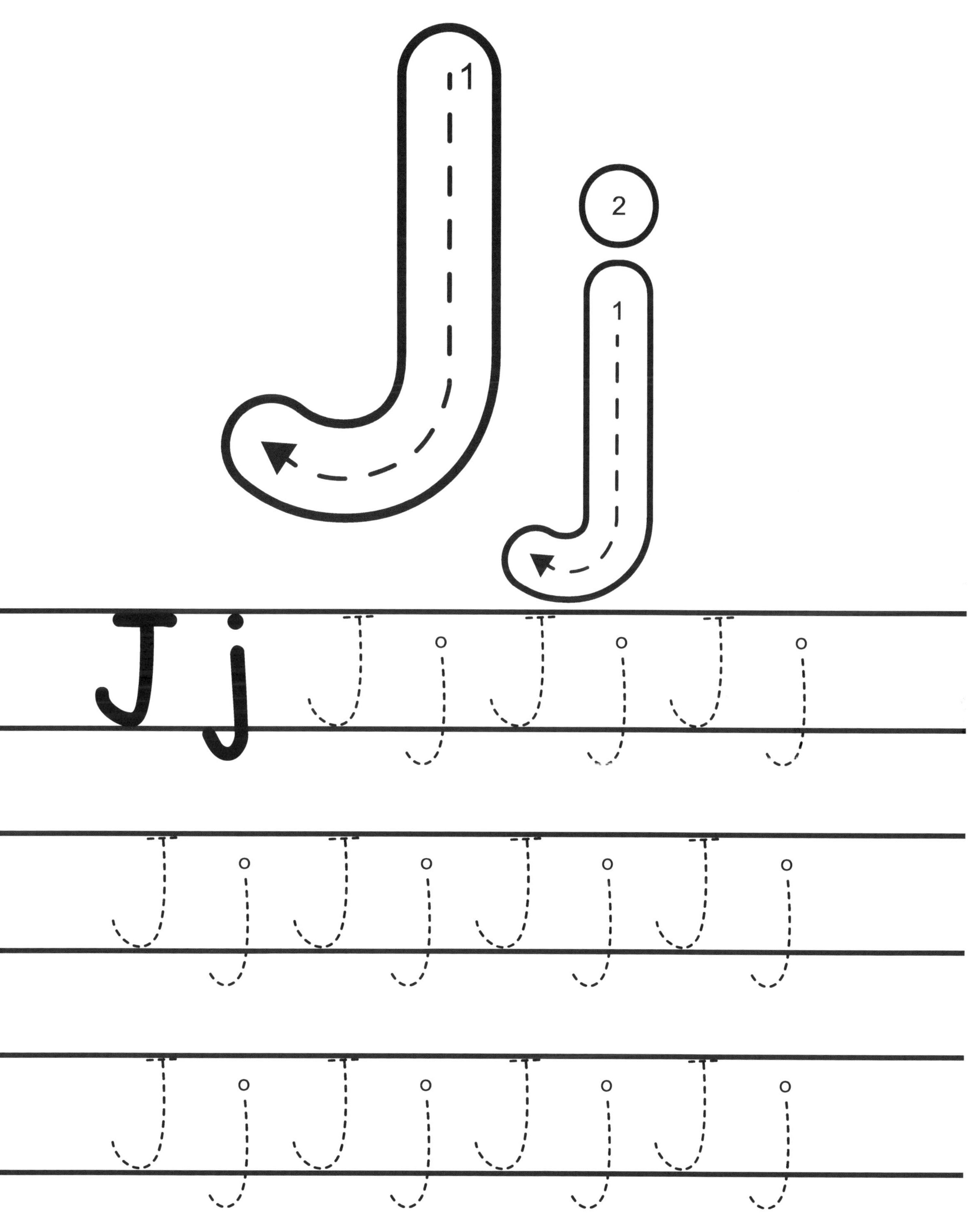

I am jubilant!
I am jubilant!
I am jubilant!

I am joyful!
I am joyful!
I am joyful!

I am clothed with the armor of God to stand against the enemy's schemes. (Ephesians 6:11)

Kk

I am kind!

I am kind!

I am kind!

I am

knowledgeable!

I am

knowledgeable!

I AM A LIGHT
IN A WORLD
OF DARKNESS.
(MATTHEW 5:16)

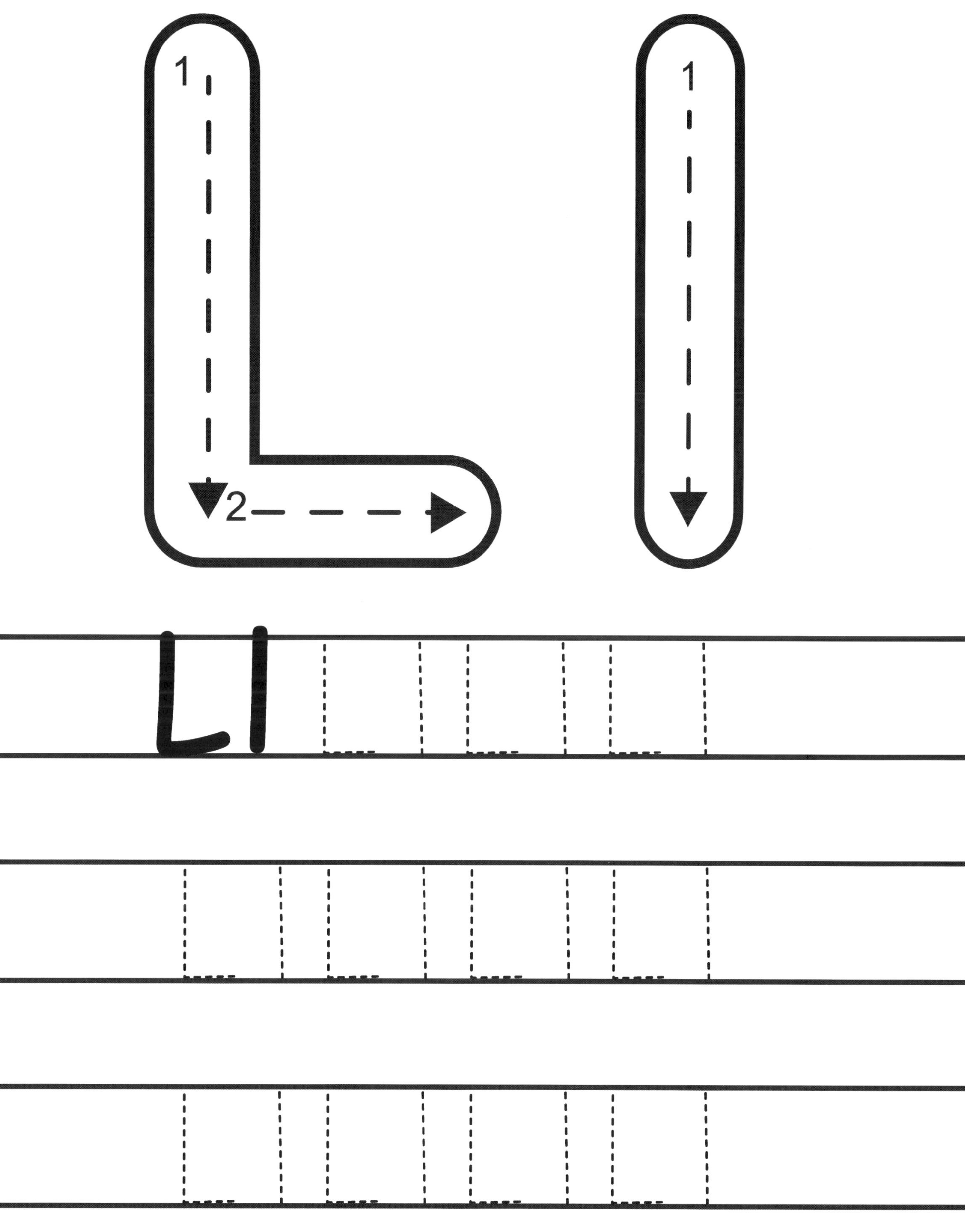
1
2
1
Ll

I am lovable!

I am lovable!

I am lovable!

I am a leader!

I am a leader!

I am a leader!

I am confident
that God's plans
for me are
good and filled
with hope.
(Jeremiah 29:11)

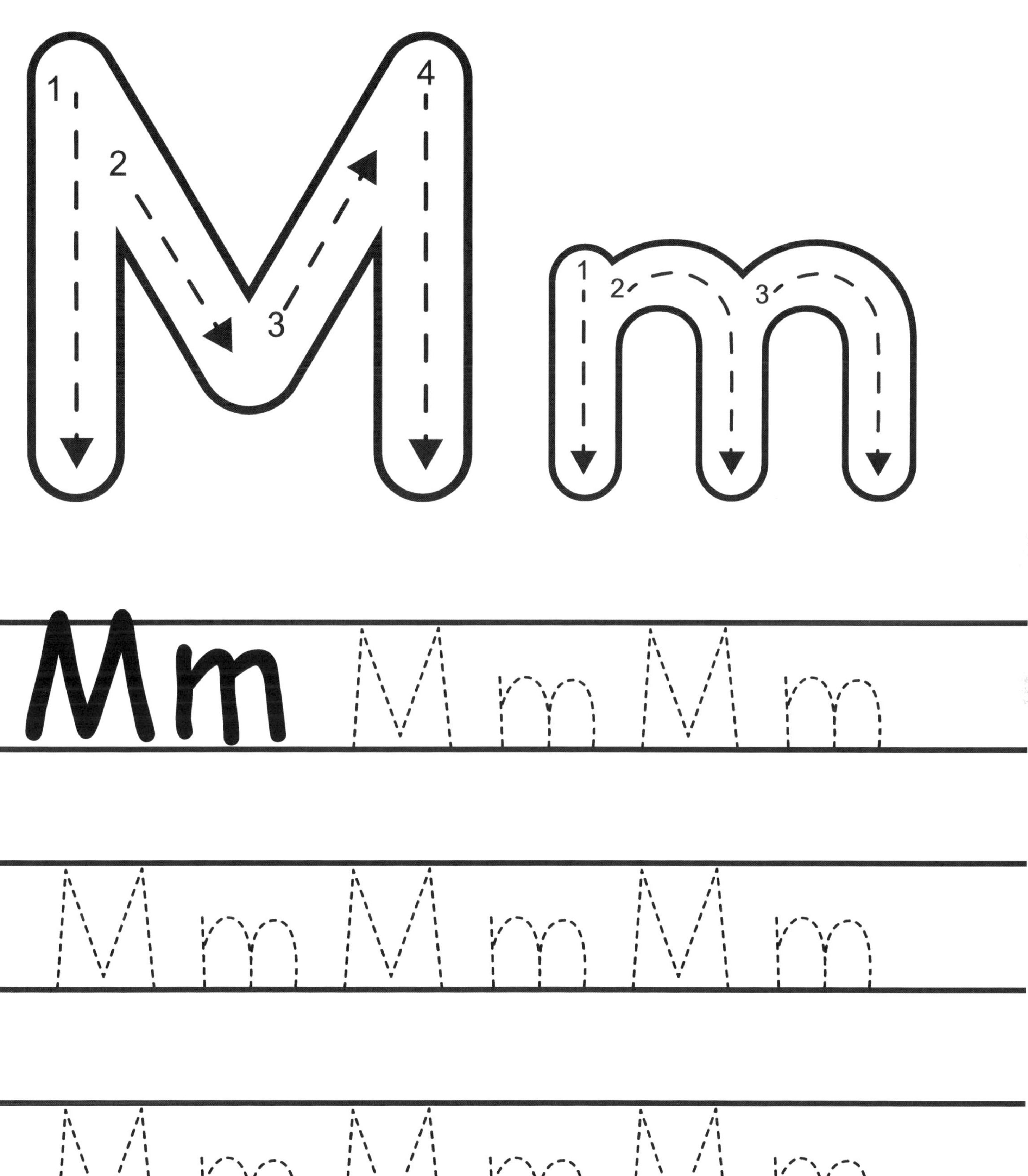
1
2
3
4
1
2
3
Mm

I am mighty!

I am mighty!

I am mighty!

I am marvelous!

I am marvelous!

I am marvelous!

I am anointed by the Holy Spirit to proclaim the Good News. (Luke 4:18)

1
2
3
1
2
Nn

I am nice!

I am nice!

I am nice!

I am necessary!

I am necessary!

I am necessary!

I am an overcomer through the blood of the Lamb. (Revelation 12:11)

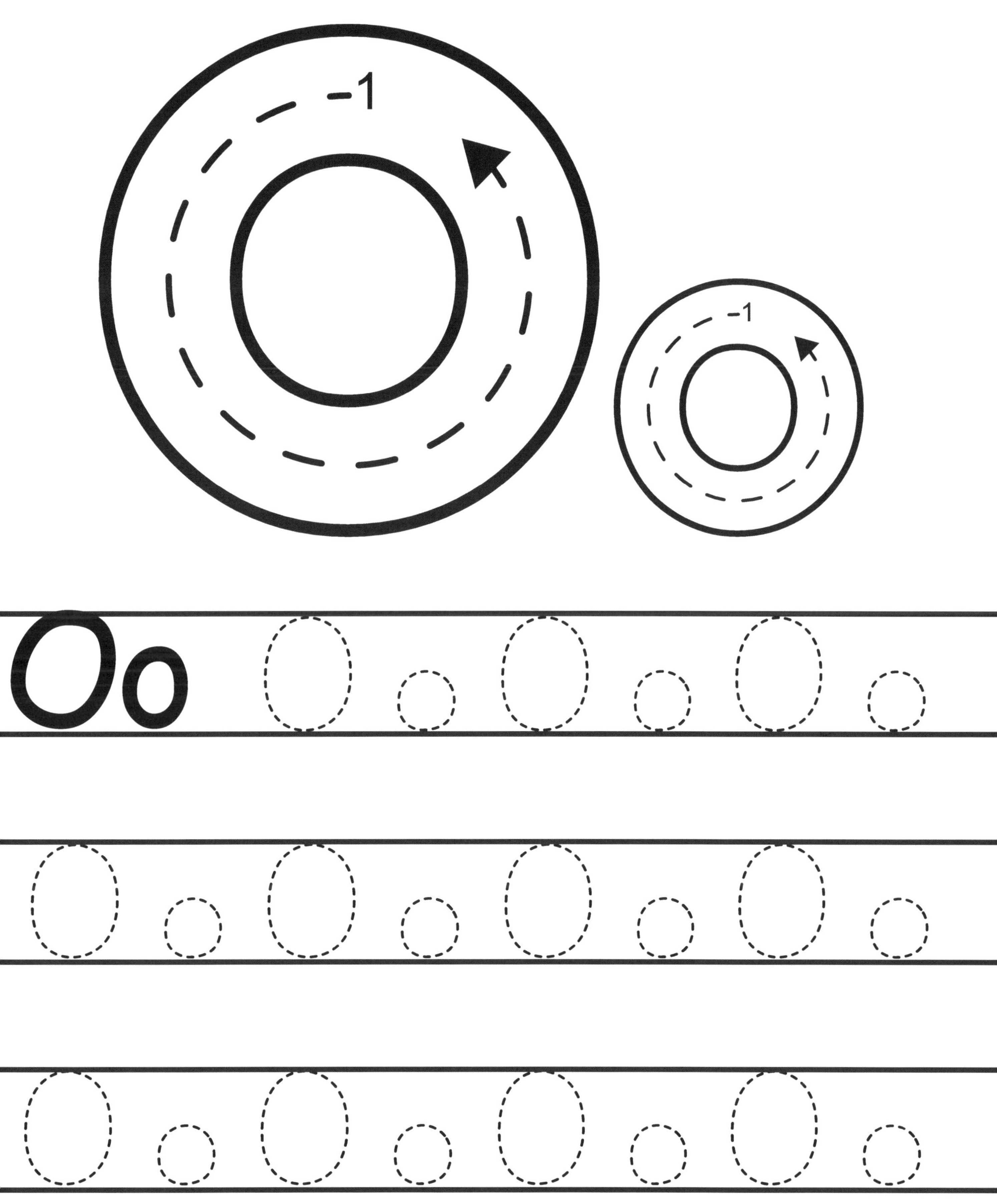

1
1
Oo

I am original!
I am original!
I am original!

I am optimistic!

I am optimistic.

I am optimistic.

I AM A
PEACEMAKER,
CALLED A
CHILD OF GOD.
(MATTHEW 5:9)

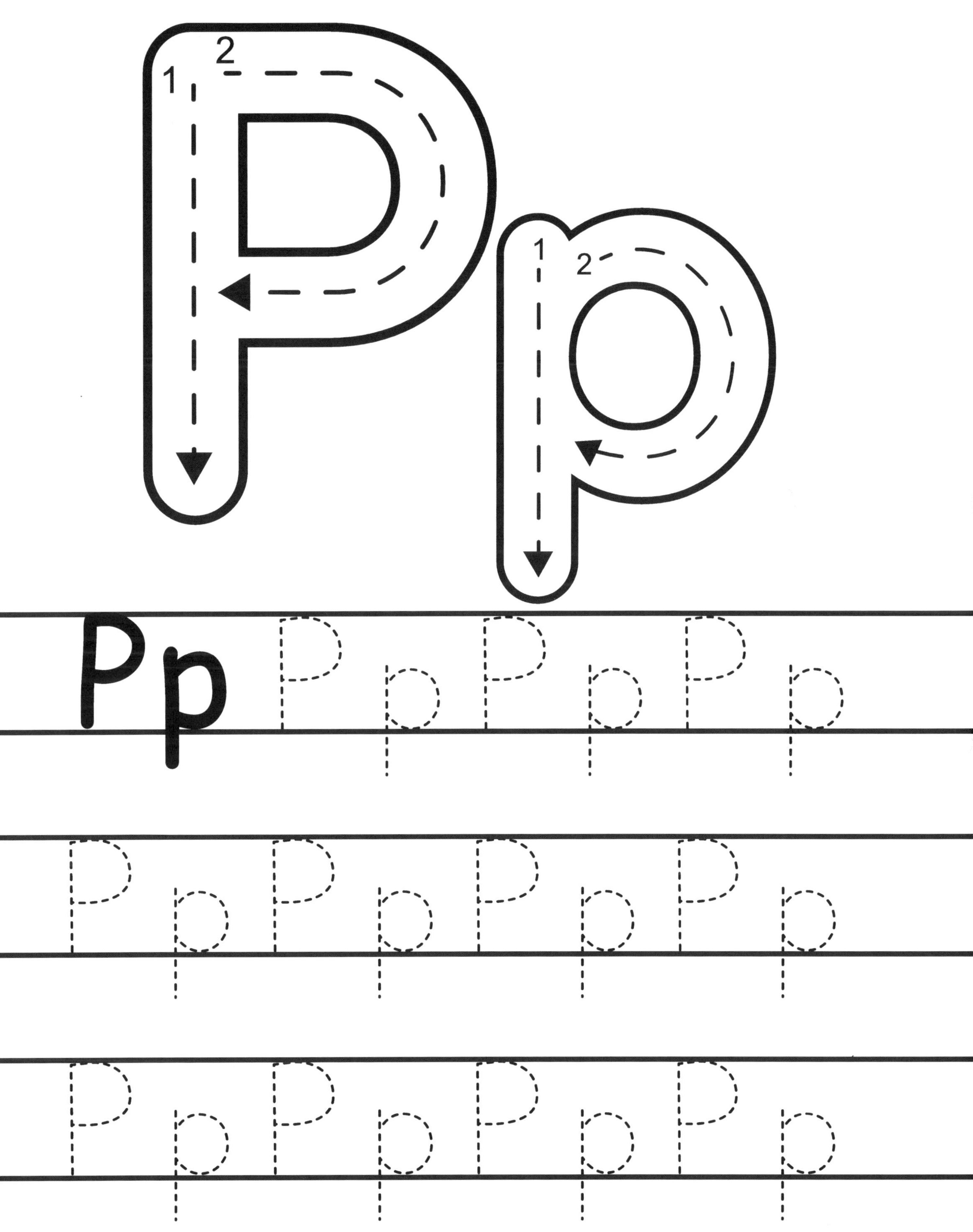
1
2
1
2
Pp

I am phenomenal!

I am phenomenal!

I am phenomenal!

I am peaceful!

I am peaceful!

I am peaceful!

I am filled with joy and peace through faith in Christ. (Romans 15:13)

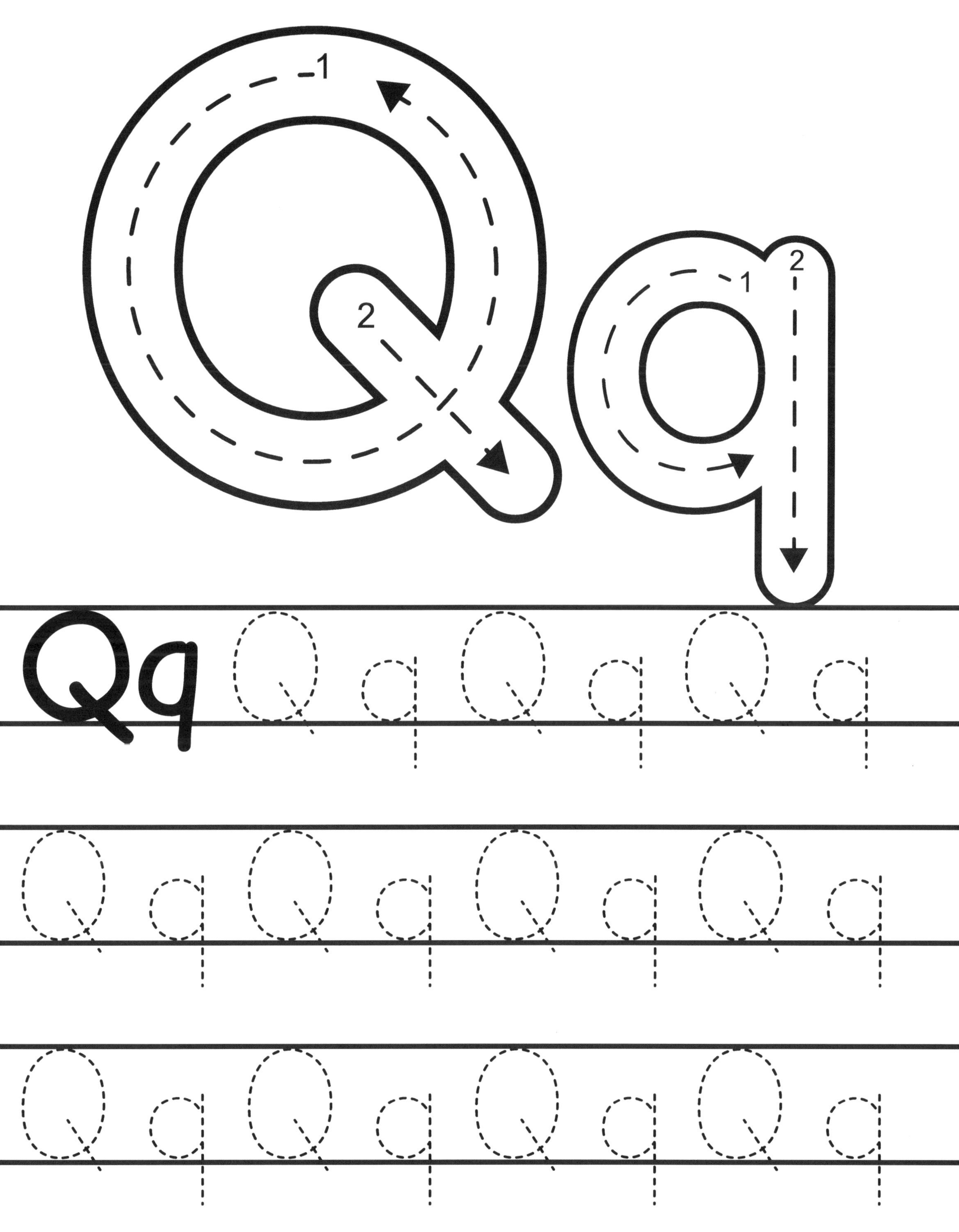
1
2
1
2
Qq

I am quiet!
I am quiet!
I am quiet!

I am quick!
I am quick!
I am quick!

I am rooted
and established
in God's love.
(Ephesians 3:17)

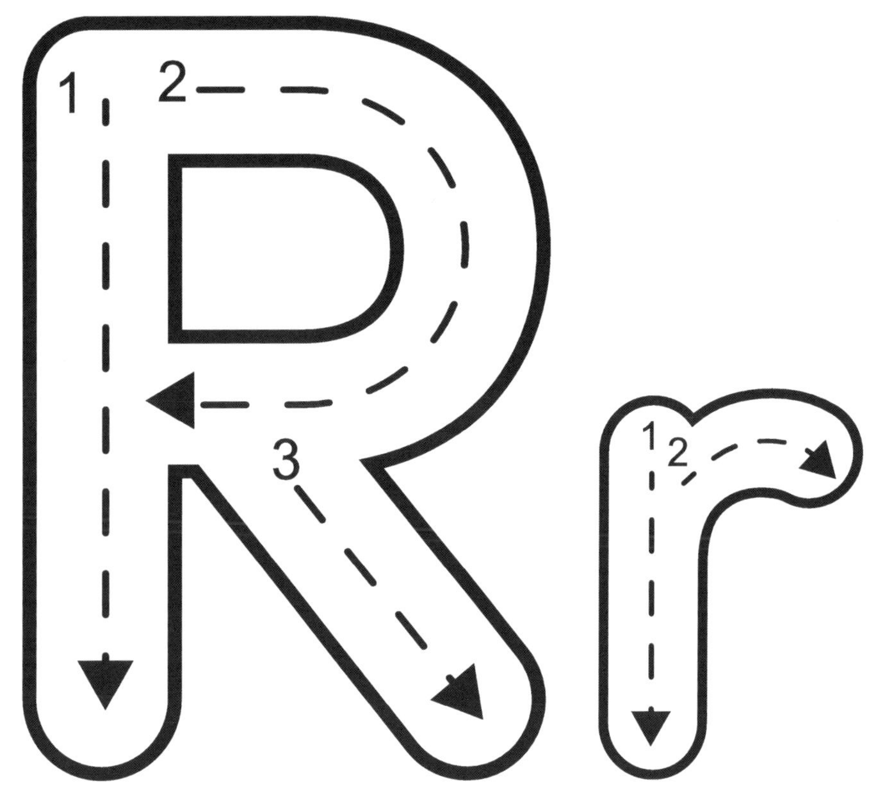

Rr R r R r R r

R r R r R r R r

R r R r R r R r

I am respectful!

I am respectful!

I am respectful!

I am radiant!

I am radiant!

I am radiant!

I AM A LIVING
SACRIFICE,
HOLY AND PLEASING
TO GOD.
(ROMANS 12:1)

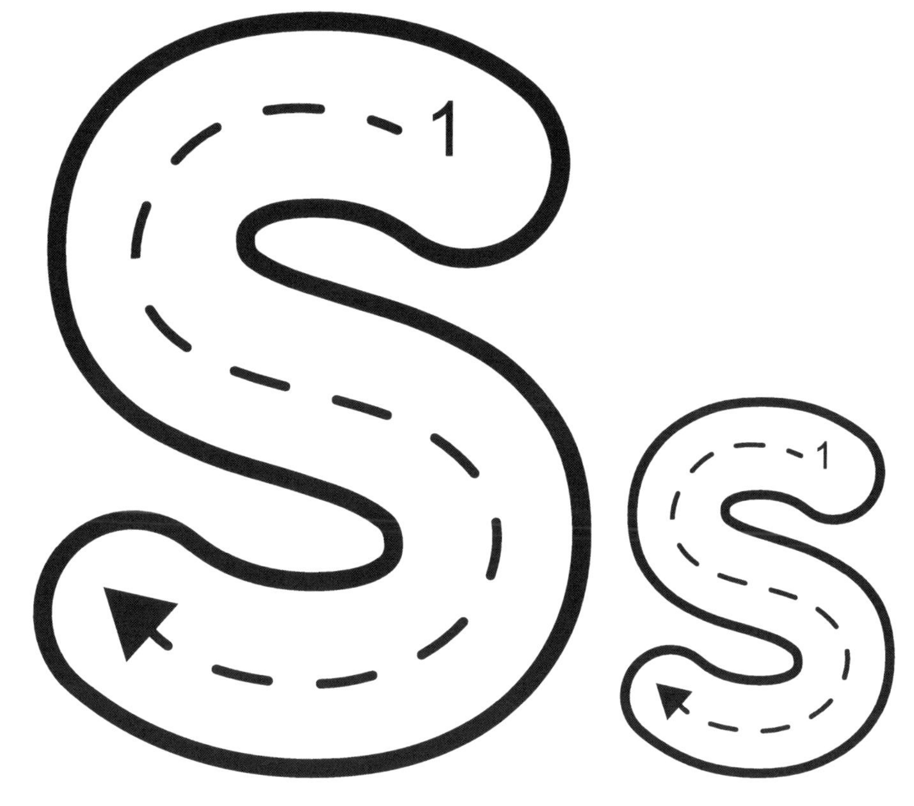

Ss

I am smart!

I am smart!

I am smart!

I am strong!

I am strong!

I am strong!

I AM A TEMPLE
OF THE
LIVING GOD.
(2 CORINTHIANS 6:16)

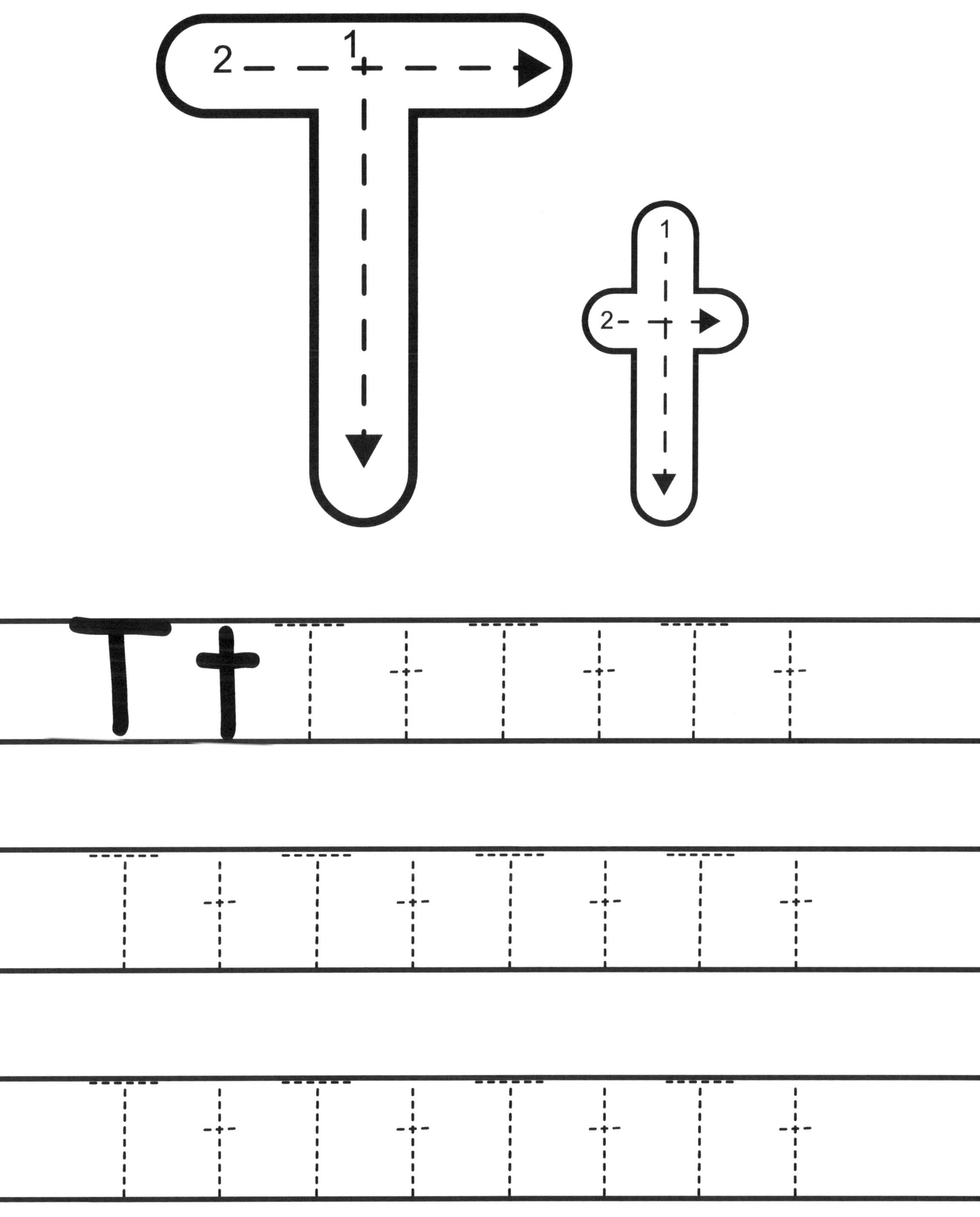
1
2
1
2
T t

I am terrific!

I am terrific!

I am terrific!

I am thoughtful!

I am thoughtful!

I am thoughtful!

I am an instrument of righteousness, presenting myself to God. (Romans 6:13)

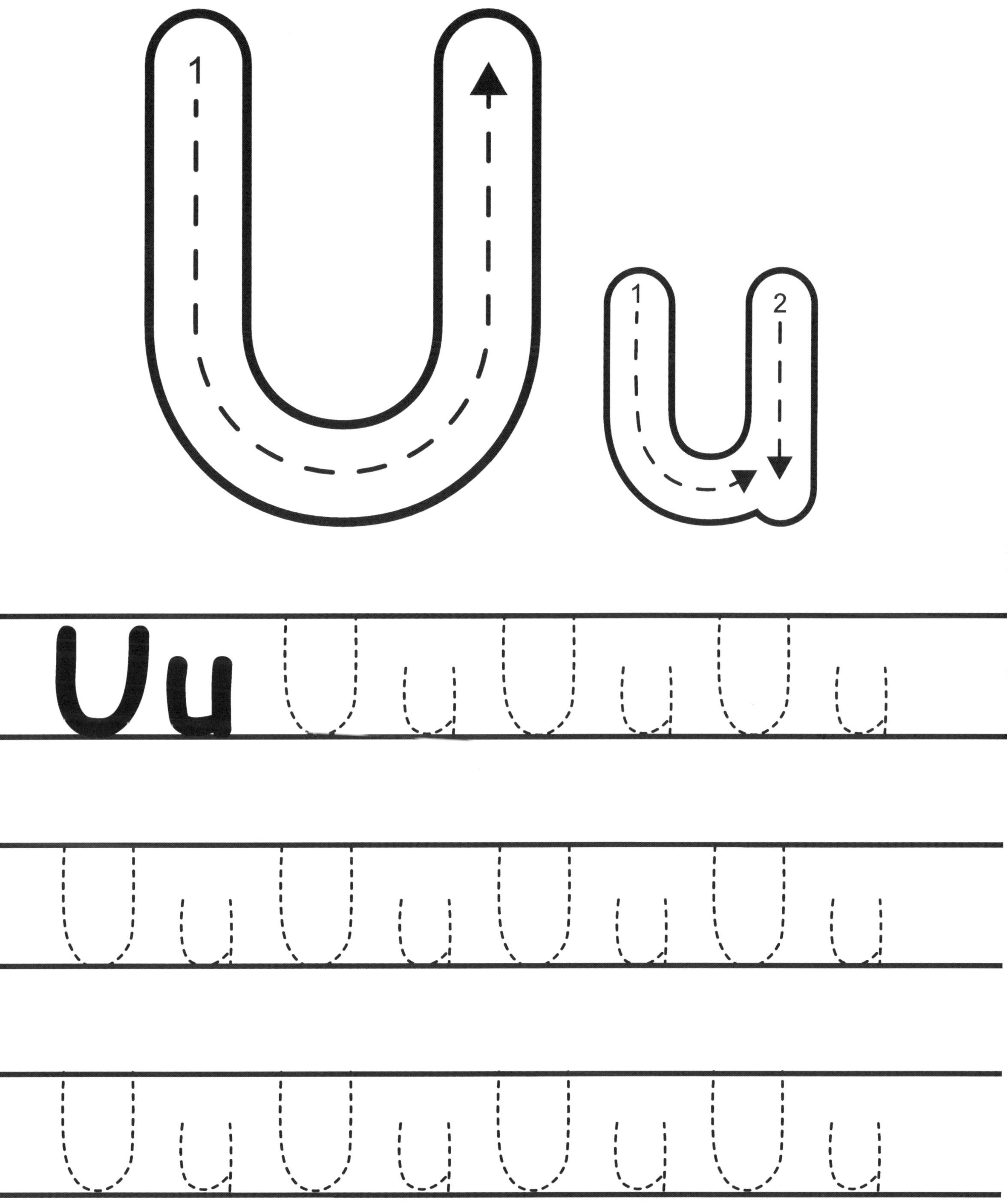

I am upstanding!

I am upstanding!

I am upstanding!

I am unique!

I am unique!

I am unique!

I AM A VESSEL
OF GOD'S
PEACE AND LOVE.
(COLOSSIANS 3:15)

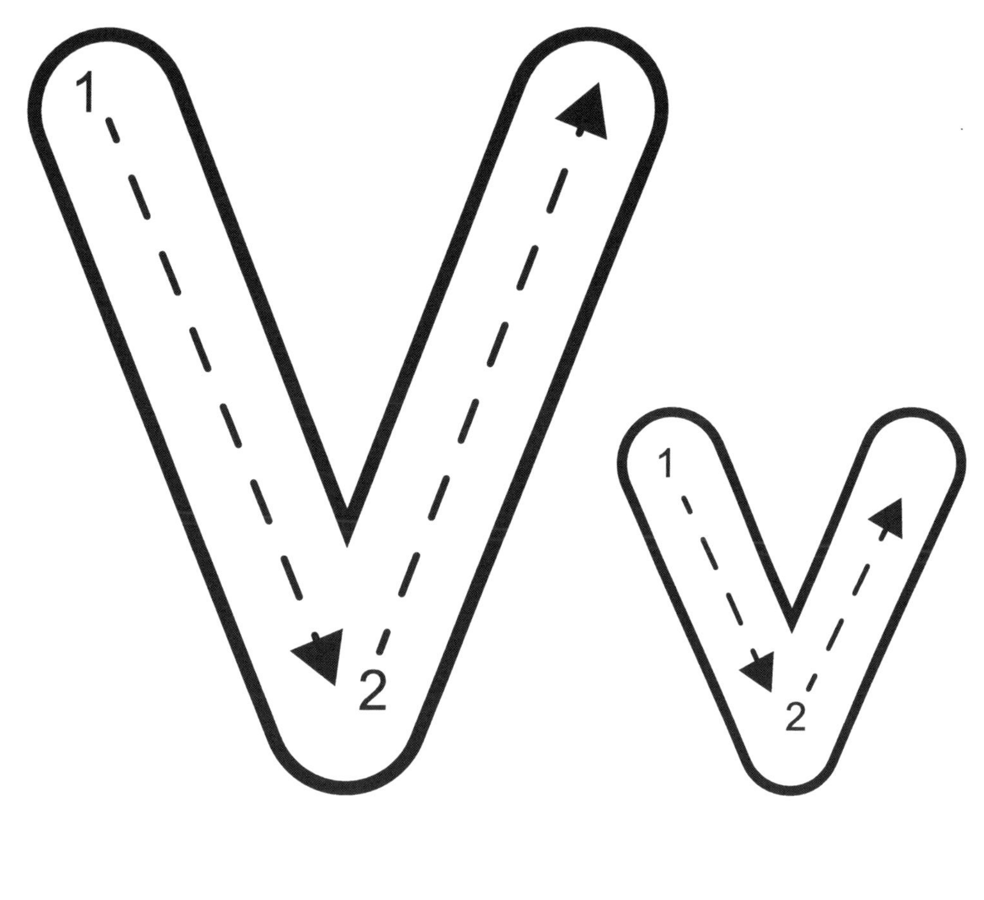

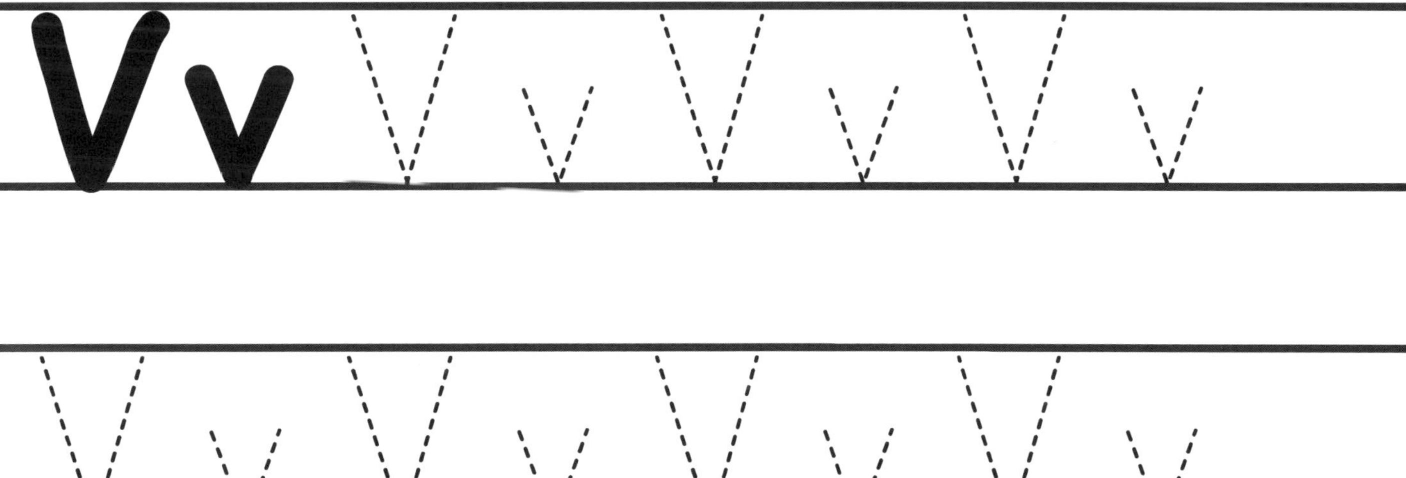
Vv

I am vibrant!

I am vibrant!

I am vibrant!

I am virtuous!

I am virtuous!

I am virtuous!

I AM WISE AND
WALK IN
THE WAYS
OF THE LORD.
(PROVERBS 13:20)

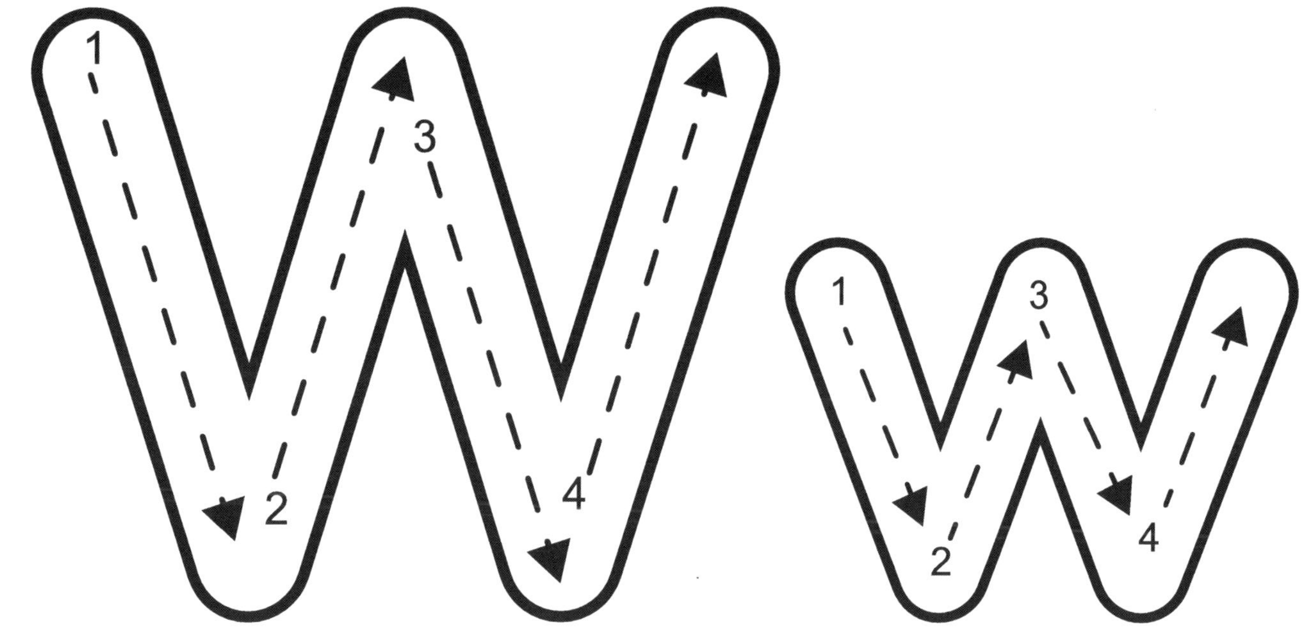

Ww

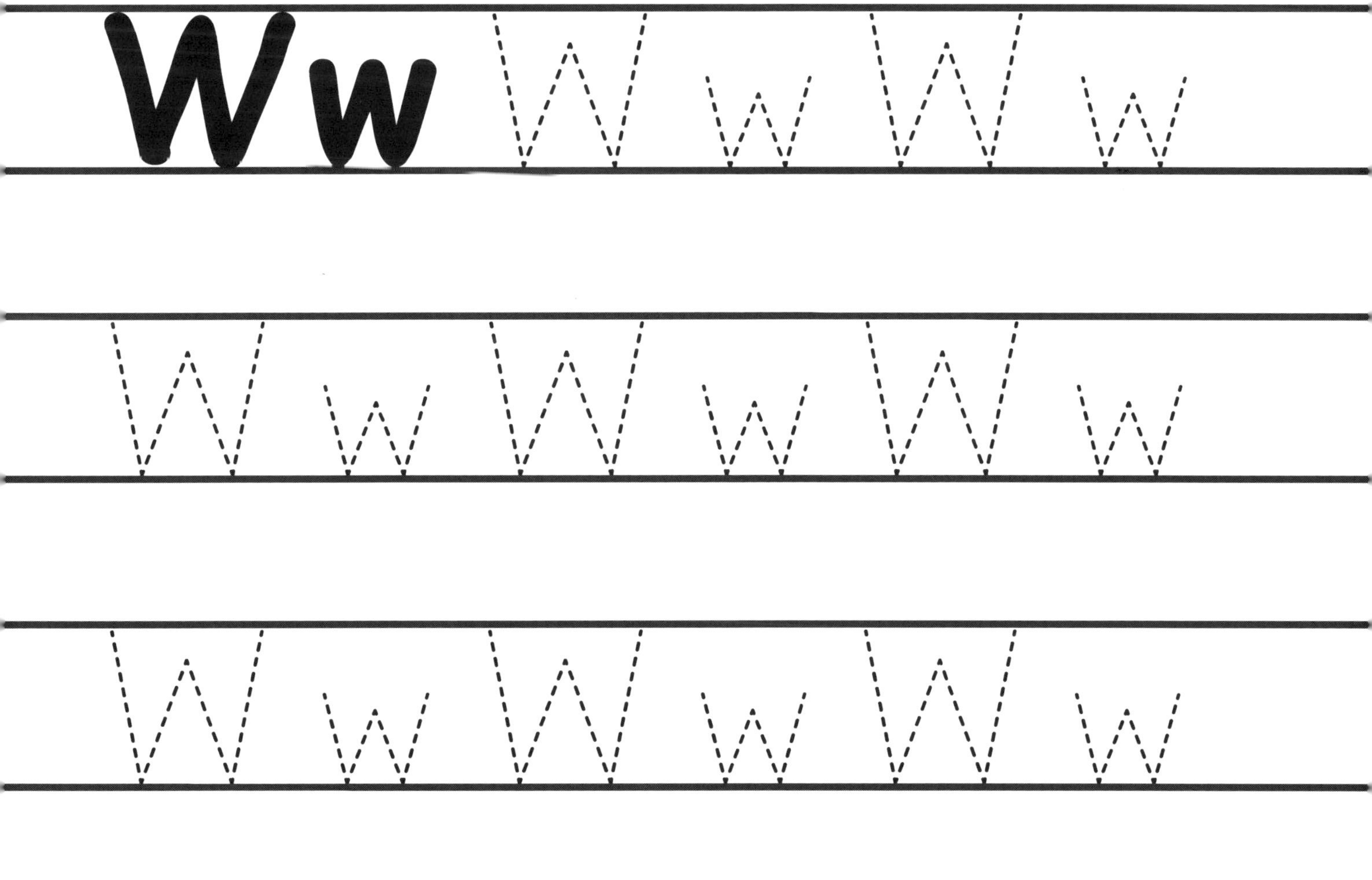

I am wonderful!

I am wonderful!

I am wonderful!

I am a winner!

I am a winner!

I am a winner!

I am God's workmanship, created for good works in Christ. (Ephesians 2:10)

1
2
1
2
Xx

I am eXuberant!

I am eXuberant!

I am eXuberant!

I am eXciting!

I am eXciting!

I am eXciting!

I am redeemed and purchased by the blood of Jesus. (Ephesians 1:7)

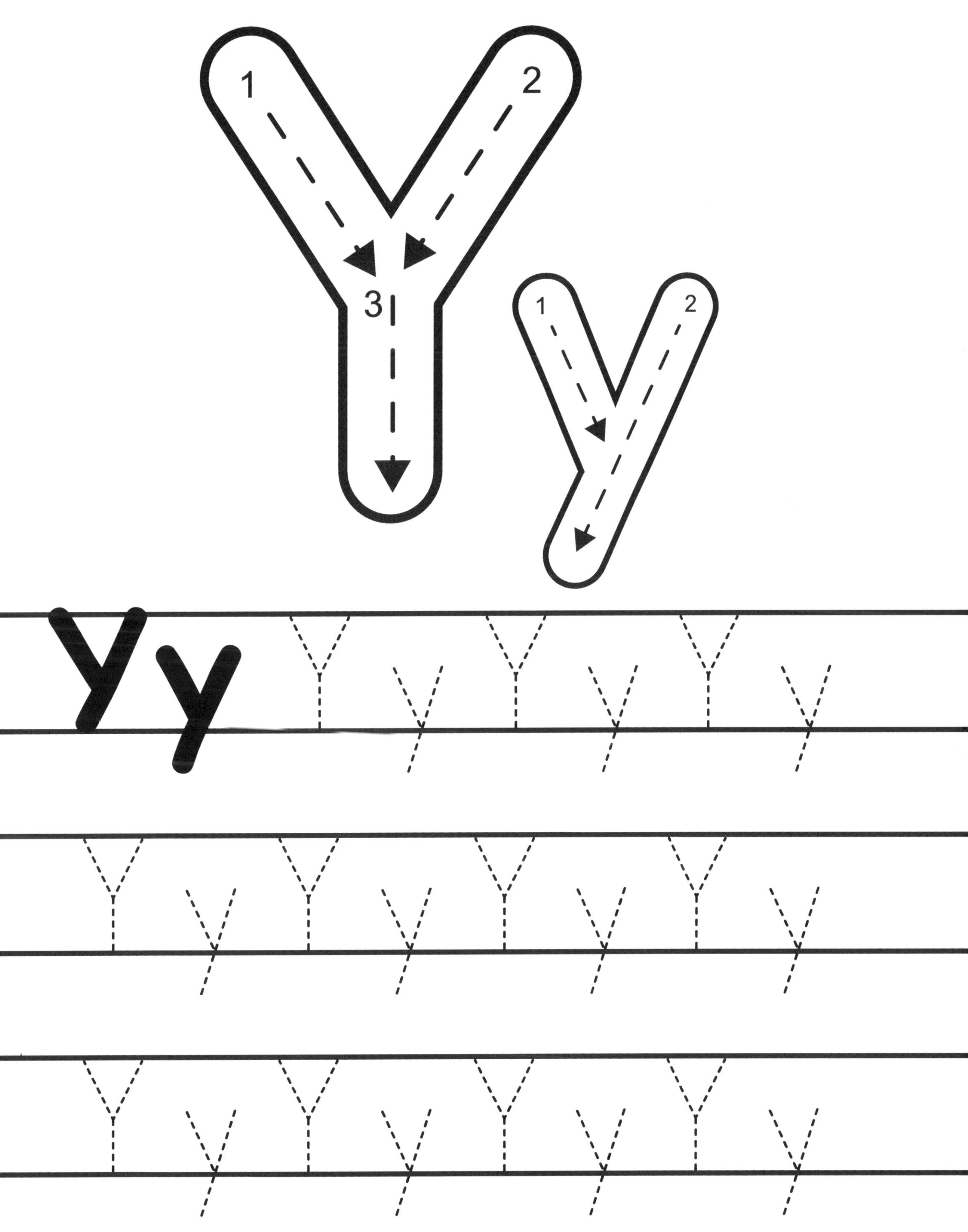
1
2
3
1
2
Yy

I am young!

I am young!

I am young!

I am youthful!

I am youthful!

I am youthful!

I am confident
that God is working
all things together
for my good.
(Romans 8:28)

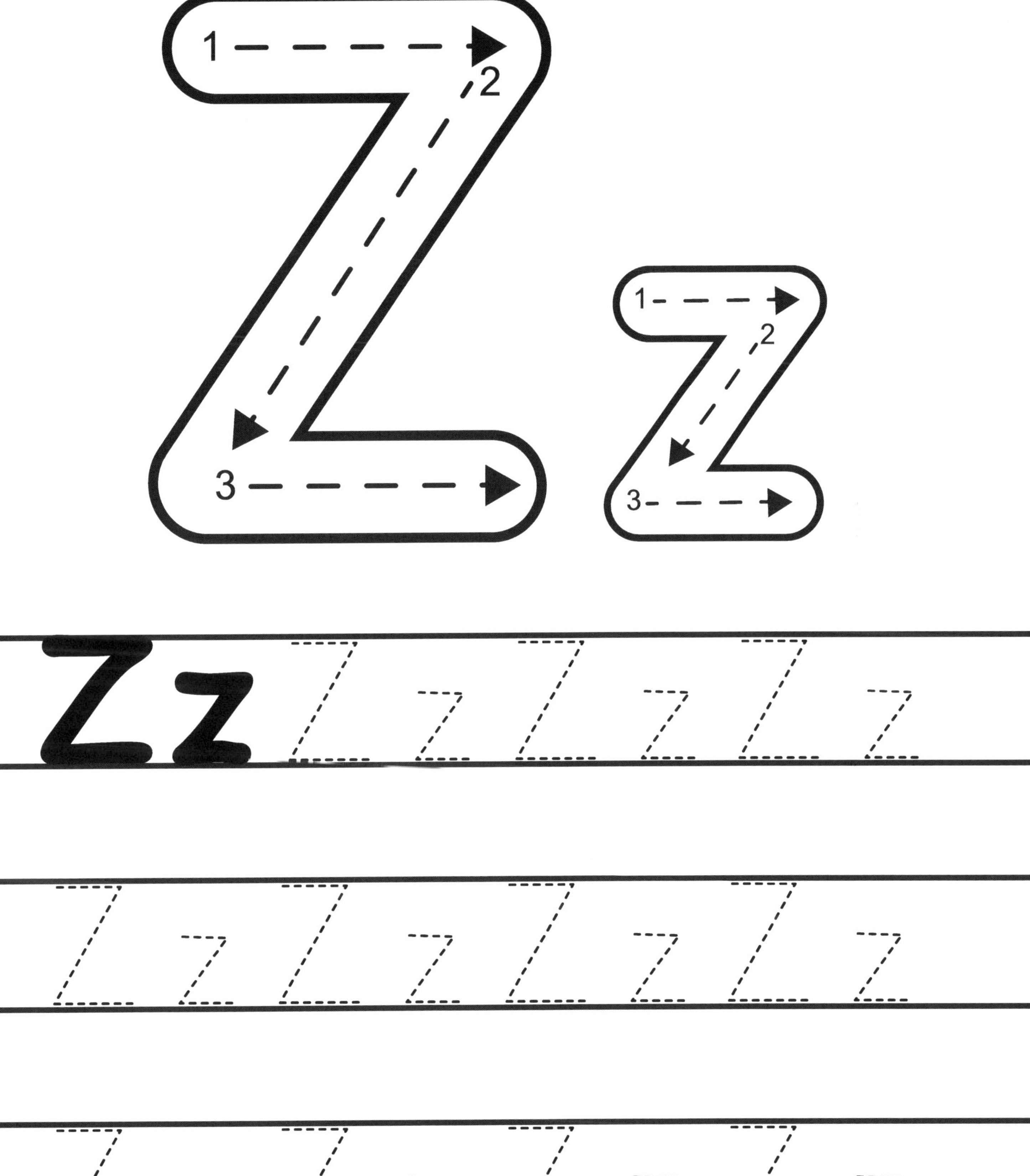

1
2
3
1
2
3
Zz

I am zealous!

I am zealous!

I am zealous!

I have zeal!

I have zeal!

I have zeal!

I am fearfully
and wonderfully
made!

Made in the USA
Middletown, DE
25 February 2025